Write, Draw & Read

SIGHT WORD MINI-BOOKS

50 Literacy-Boosting Reproducibles That Teach the Top Sight Words

Barbara Maio & Rozanne Lanczak Williams

New York • Toronto • London • Auckland • Sydney
Mexico City • New Delhi • Hong Kong • Buenos Aires

*Dedicated to all the wonderful
and talented teachers in our lives*

Editor: Liza Charlesworth
Cover design: Michelle H. Kim
Interior design: Grafica Inc.

Scholastic Inc., 557 Broadway, New York, NY 10012
ISBN: 978-1-338-30630-9
Copyright © 2019 by Barbara Maio and Rozanne Lanczak Williams
All rights reserved.
Printed in the U.S.A.
First printing, January 2019.

1 2 3 4 5 6 7 8 9 10   40   25 24 23 22 21 20 19

CONTENTS

REPRODUCIBLE MINI-BOOKS

Dear Educator,

Welcome to *Write, Draw & Read Sight Word Mini-Books*! We're a teacher-writer team and we developed these mini-books to help young learners master key sight words.

What are sight words? Sight words are those important words—*is, the, of, with, you, for, they*—that are everywhere in print, but are seldom decodable. In fact, research shows that these words comprise up to 75 percent of the texts children encounter when they read. For that reason, reading specialists advocate a variety of activities to help students commit these all-important words to memory. These easy-to-make mini-books should be a part of the mix.

Inviting children to make the mini-books and complete the open-ended prompts will help to "hardwire" more than 100 sight words. In addition, the mini-books provide rich opportunities to boost reading, writing, spelling, phonics, fluency, fine motor, critical thinking, AND comprehension skills. That's a whole lot of learning packed into a simple—and fun!—classroom activity.

Since our mini-books were tested in Barbara's classroom, we know they work wonders with new readers. So share them with your students today… and watch their literacy skills soar!

Warmly,

Barbara & Rozanne

How to Use This Book

These mini-books are designed to reinforce and practice sight words that have been previously taught or introduced in your classroom. They can be used in any sequence. They supplement any early literacy program and meet individual student needs.

1. Choose a *Write, Draw & Read Sight Word Mini-Book* (or use pages 58–64 to create your own mini-book). Reproduce it for students.

2. Cut the page along the solid line. Then fold it along the dashed lines to make a four-page mini-book.

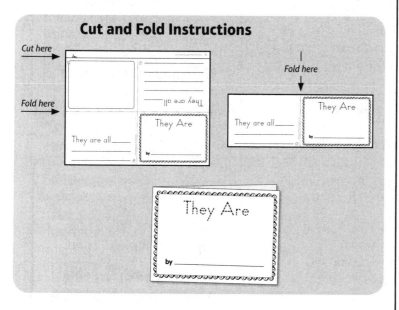

Cut and Fold Instructions

3. Gather a small group of students, each with a pre-folded mini-book.

4. Read aloud the mini-book title phrase as you point to each word. Have students read the phrase together. Then, ask students, one-by-one, to read the phrase while pointing to the words.

5. Trace the dotted letters in the title as you say each word in the phrase. Have students finger-trace the dotted letters as they say each word (imitating the teacher).

Great Reasons to ♡ *Write, Draw & Read Sight Word Mini-Books:*

- **They Reinforce Must-Know Sight Words** Children will build fluency by practicing these sight words in phrases and meaningful contexts.

- **They Allow for Differentiated Learning** Because the phrases are open-ended, children can write at their own developmental levels.

- **They Motivate and Inspire Beginning Writers** Since the stories allow for individual choice, children feel empowered to truly express themselves.

- **They Boost Key Phonics and Spelling Skills** As children sound out words and use temporary spelling to complete their mini-books, they develop and apply essential literacy skills.

- **They Build Higher Levels of Comprehension** Using these phrases to create their own stories enables children to build higher-level comprehension skills.

- **They Promote Independence** Once children are familiar with the format, they will be able to complete the mini-books independently.

- **They Can Be Integrated Across the Curriculum** The mini-books can be used to enrich many curricular themes and concepts.

- **They Connect School to Home** The mini-books provide engaging opportunities to write, draw, and read in school or at home.

6. Read the title again and ask, "What could this book be about?" Lead a discussion, soliciting student ideas for what to include in the book and modeling how to add details and/or expand the sentences.

TIP: The mini-books can be used to enrich curricular themes and concepts by adding words to the title.

EXAMPLE
Here Is a Mammal
Here is a fox.
Here is a bear.

7. Ask students to look at the inside pages. Encourage them to expand a one-word response by asking questions or offering suggestions for completing their sentences and extending their ideas. By listening to others in the group explain and expand on their own sentences or ideas, students "get ideas" to try. Students could also talk with partners who can offer suggestions.

TIP: Have students look at the last page of the mini-book. There may be an added sight word to make the story more interesting. Discuss with students ways to finish their stories.

8. Invite children to return to their desks to independently complete their mini-books and remind them to illustrate the pages.

TIP: It is important to encourage students to use temporary or phonetic spelling for all other words they write. We've found this results in more sophisticated and vivid writing.

9. Students can share their completed mini-books with a partner or adult volunteer, and then add them to their book boxes for independent reading.

10. Use the Sight Word Phrases Assessment (see page 57) for assessment and/or send it home for extra practice.

Connection to the Standards

The mini-books support the standards for Reading Foundational Skills for students in grades K–2.

Foundational Skills
Read common high-frequency words by sight.

Print Concepts
Demonstrate understanding of the organization and basic features of print.

Phonological Awareness
Demonstrate understanding of spoken words, syllables, and sounds (phonemes).

Fluency
Read with sufficient accuracy and fluency to support comprehension.

Speaking and Listening
Participate in collaborative conversations about age-appropriate topics.

Writing
Use a combination of drawing, dictating, and writing to communicate an event or story.

I can
_____

I Can

by _____

I can
_____

I can
_____

It is ___

It is ___

②

It is ___

③

It is ___

by ___

④

I am _____

_____

_____

②

I Am

by _____

④

I am _____

_____

_____

I am _____

③

I am _____

They are all _____

②

They Are

by _____

④

They are all _____

③

I like _____

_____

_____

②

I like _____

_____

_____

③

_____

_____

_____

I like _____

④

I don't like _____

_____

_____

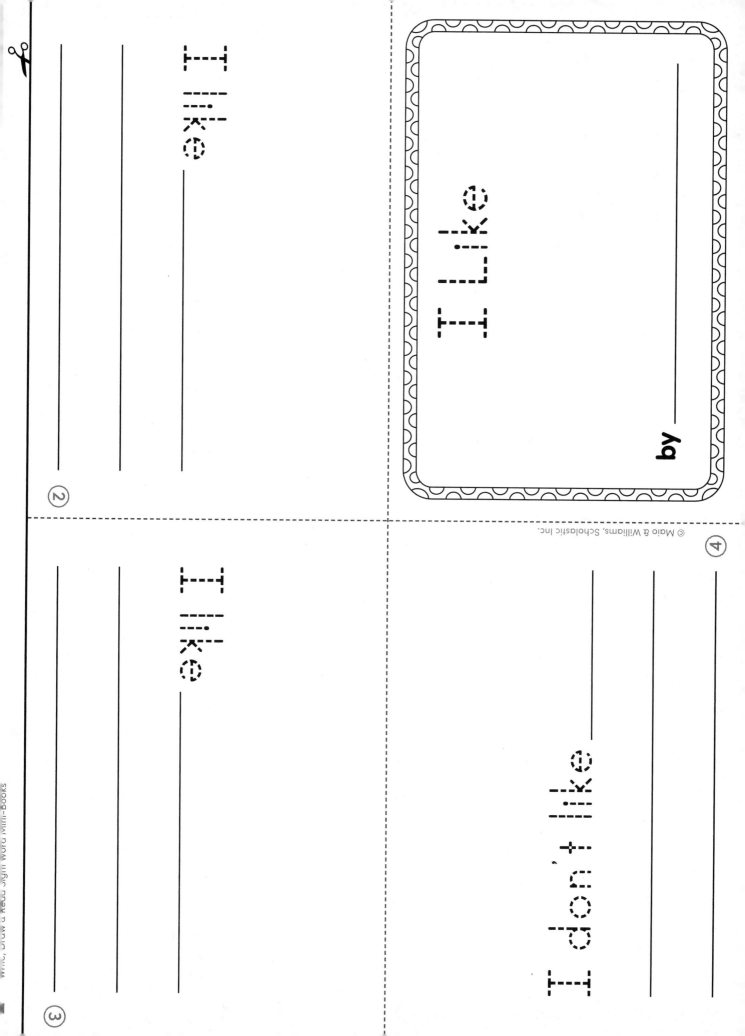

I Like _____

by _____

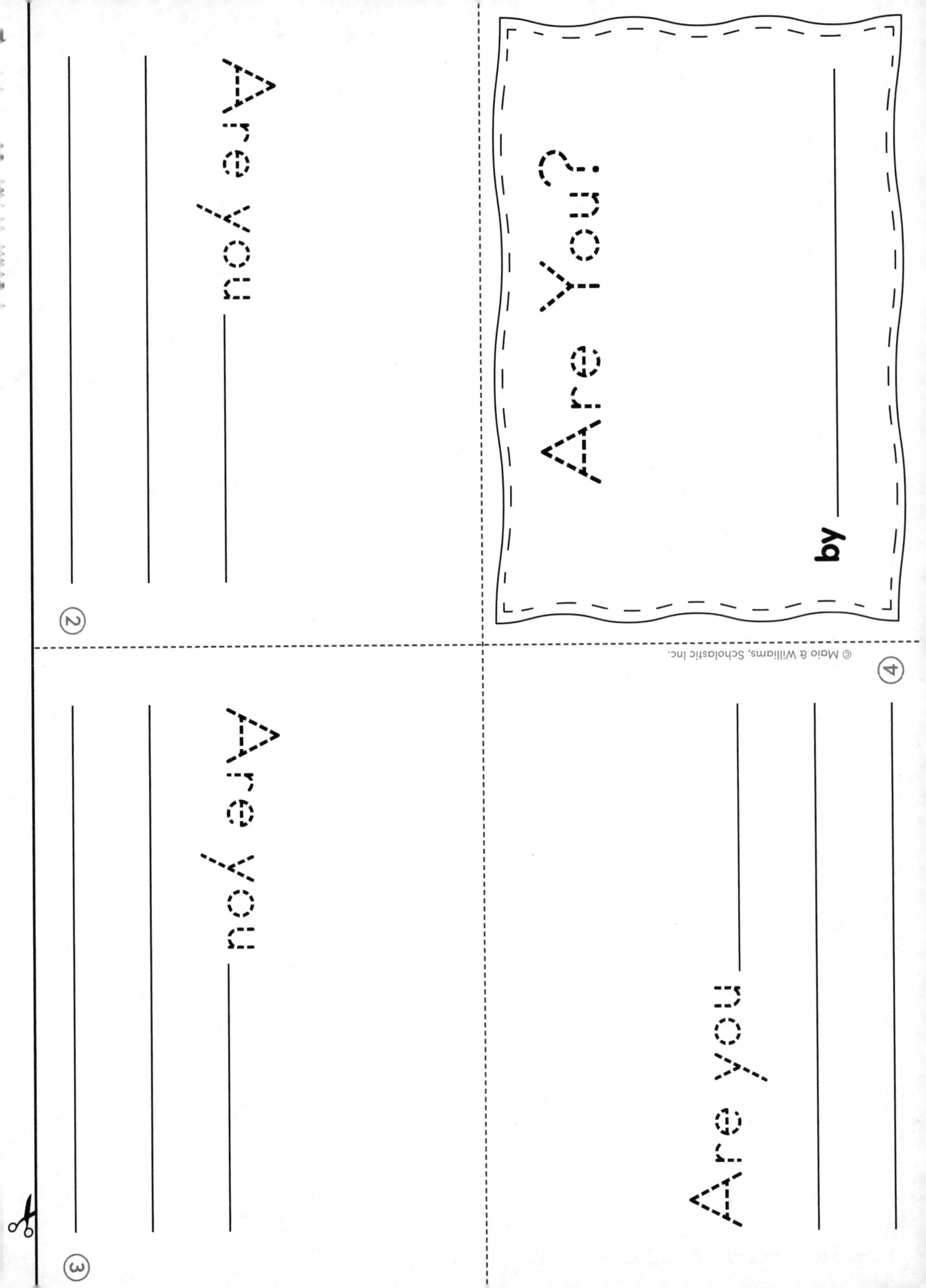

I see the _____

②

I See

by _____

④

I see the _____

③

I see the _____

③

He can go

4

He can go

© Maio & Williams, Scholastic Inc.

2

He can go

He Can Go

by ____

He can go

③

Come and get

④

②

Come and get

Come and Get

by _____

Here Is _____

by _____

② Here is a _____

③ Here is a _____

④ Here is a _____

③

And do you like

④

②

Do you like

Do You Like?

by

I will be

I will be

③

I will be

I will be

②

I Will Be

by

④

It is in

_____

② _____

It is in

③ _____

It is in

It Is In

by _____

④

She was
_____

She was
_____
_____

She was
_____

She Was

by
_____

Write, Draw & Read Sight Word Mini-Books

③

We have

We have

④

We have

②

We Have

by

We have

③

If You ____

____

____

②

If You ____

____

____

④

But if you ____

____

____

If You

by ____

Write, Draw & Read Sight Word Mini-Books

② Look at my _____

③ Look at my _____

④ Look at my _____

Look At

by _____

They were _____

②

_____

They Were

by _____

© Maio & Williams, Scholastic Inc.

④

They were _____

They were _____

③

This is his

This is his

③

②

④

This Is

by _____

This is his

That Is My

by ____

That is my ____

①

②

③

That is my ____

④

Where is the ___

④

③

②

Where is the ___

Where?

by ___

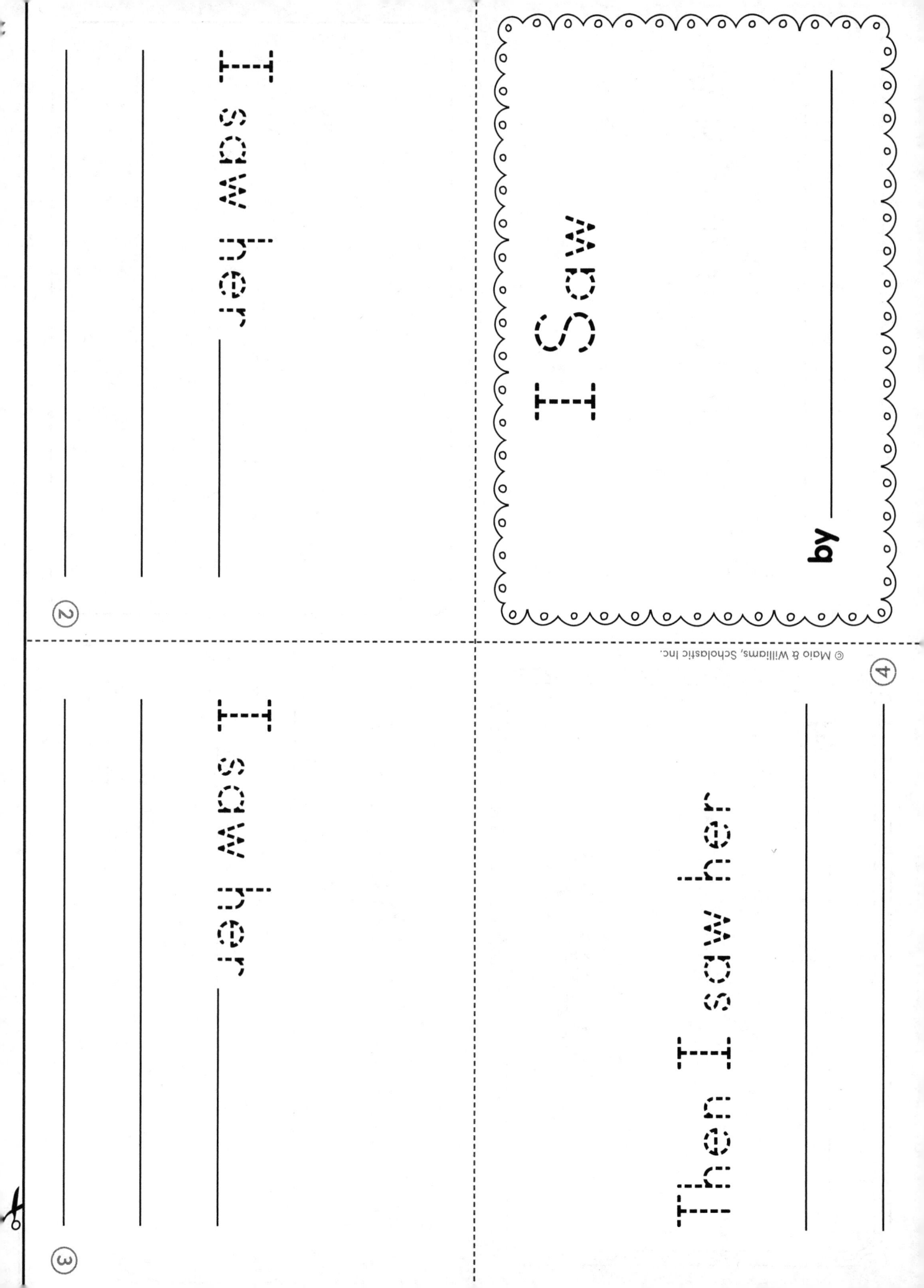

I saw

I saw her

②

I saw I

I saw her

③

Then I saw her

by

④

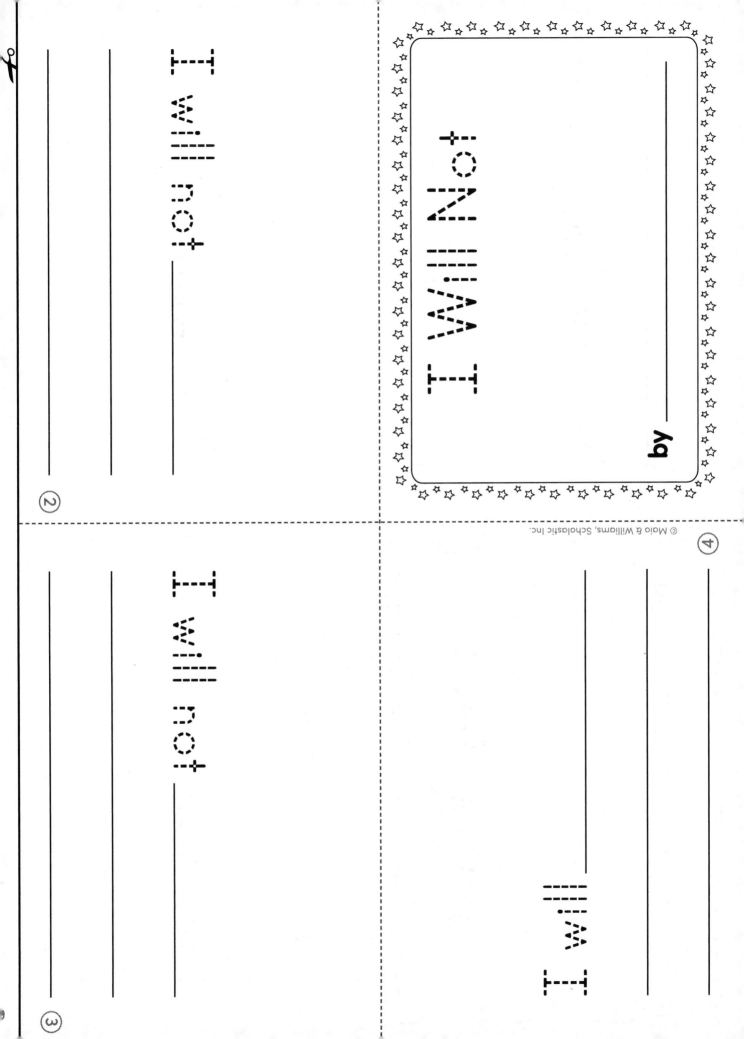

I will not ②

I will not ③

I Will NOT

by

© Maio & Williams, Scholastic Inc. ④

I will

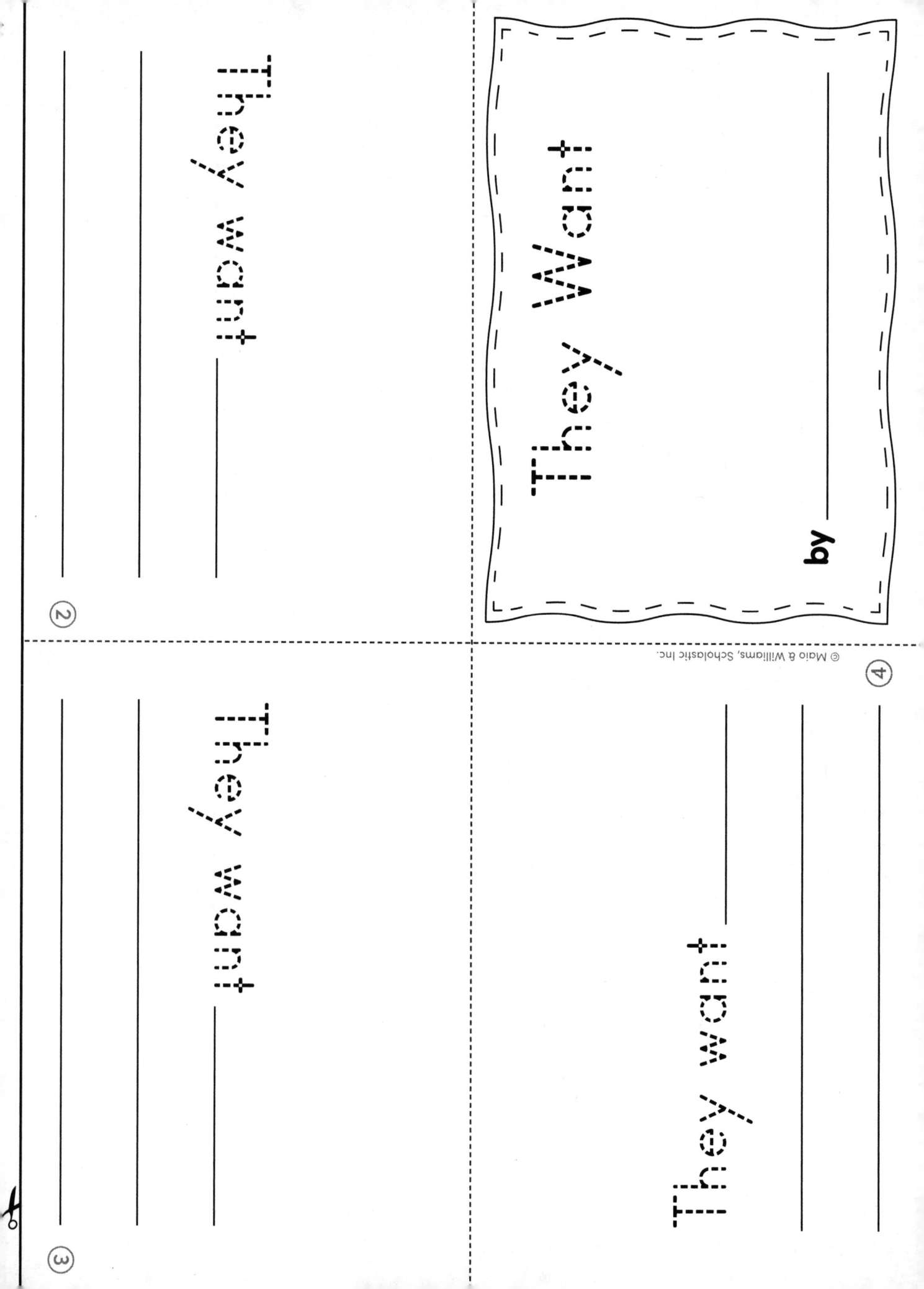

They want ____

② They want ____

They Want

by ____

④ They want ____

③ They want ____

These are for _____

④

③

②

These are for _____

These Are

by _____

We ran from ‑‑‑

We Ran

by ‑‑‑

We ran from ‑‑‑

We ran from ‑‑‑

④

How do you _____

③

②

How do you _____

How Do You?

by _____

One day I

③

One day I

②

One day I

④

One Day

by ____

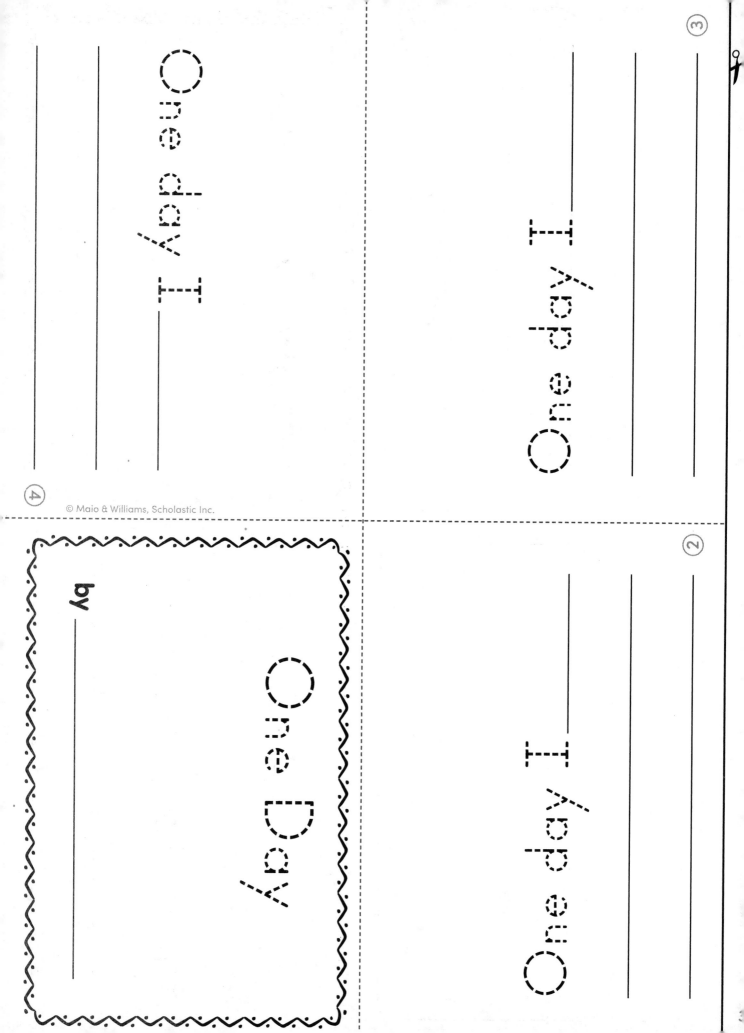

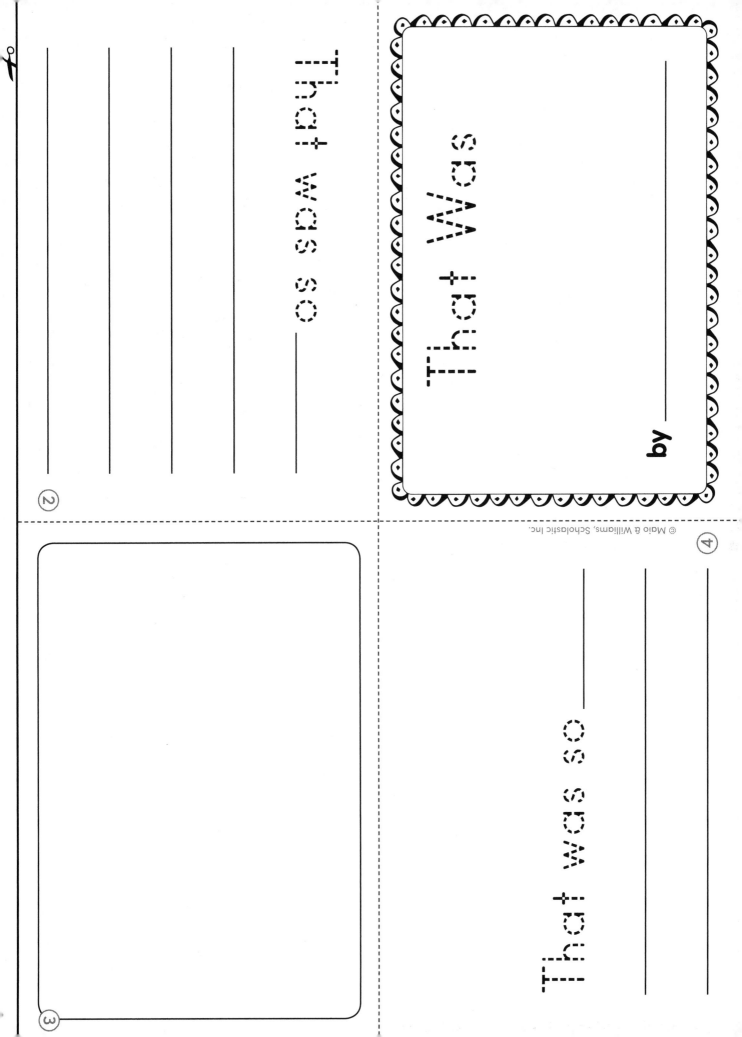

That Was

by ____

That was so ____

That was so ____

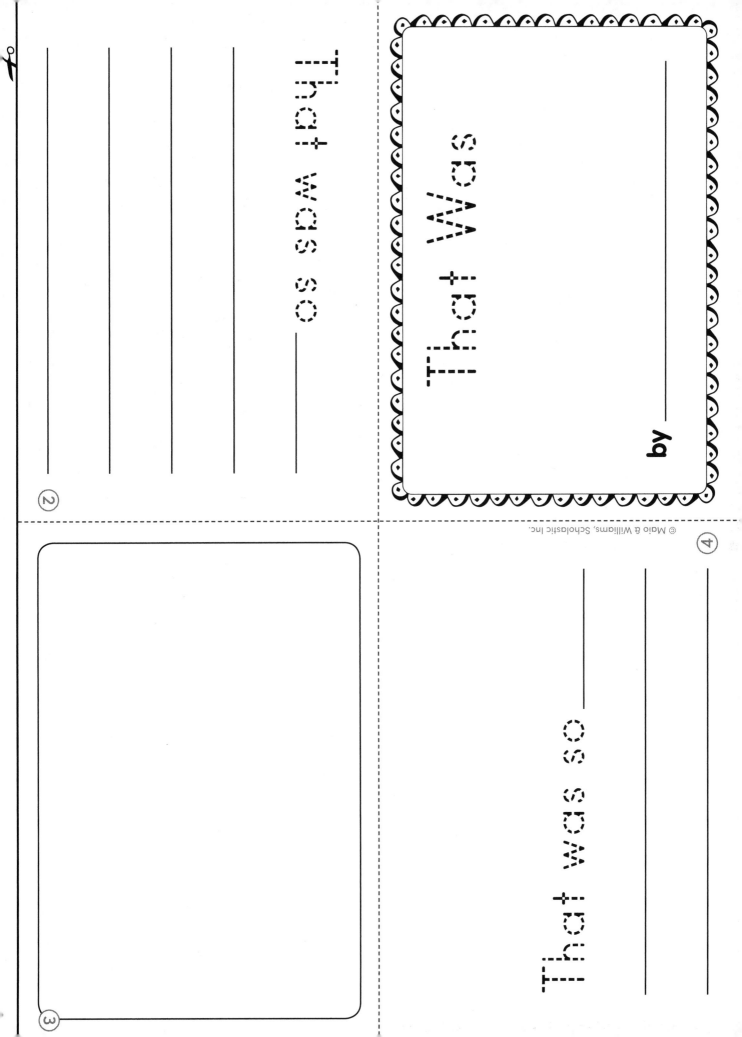

② ③ ④

We Went

by ____

2

We went into ____

3

4

© Maia & Williams, Scholastic Inc.

We went into ____

③

Your mom said...

②

Your mom said...

④

© Maio & Williams, Scholastic Inc.

Your mom said...

Your Mom Said...

by ___

Your mom said...

We can use _____

We can use _____

We Can Use

by _____

We can use _____

When can we _____

④

③

②

When can we _____

When Can We?

by _____

When can we _____

It is time

It is time ☺

It is time ☺

It is time

by _____

It is time ☺

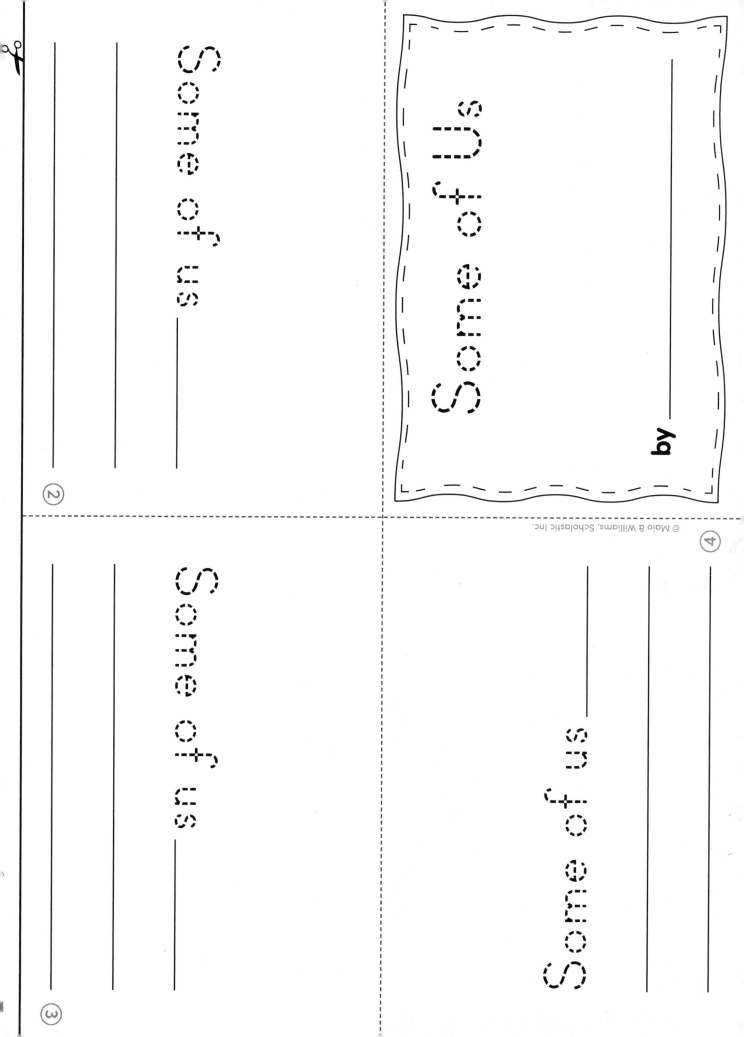

Some of us

Some of us

Some of us

Some of us

by

②

③

④

They Had Some

by ____________________

They had some ______

4

They had some ______

2

3

③

He did not

He did not

He did not

②

He did not

He did not

④

He Did Not

by _____

What is on _____

What is _____

© Maio & Williams, Scholastic Inc.

What is on _____

What is on _____

What Is?

by _____

There Are

by _____

② There are two _____

③

④ There are two _____

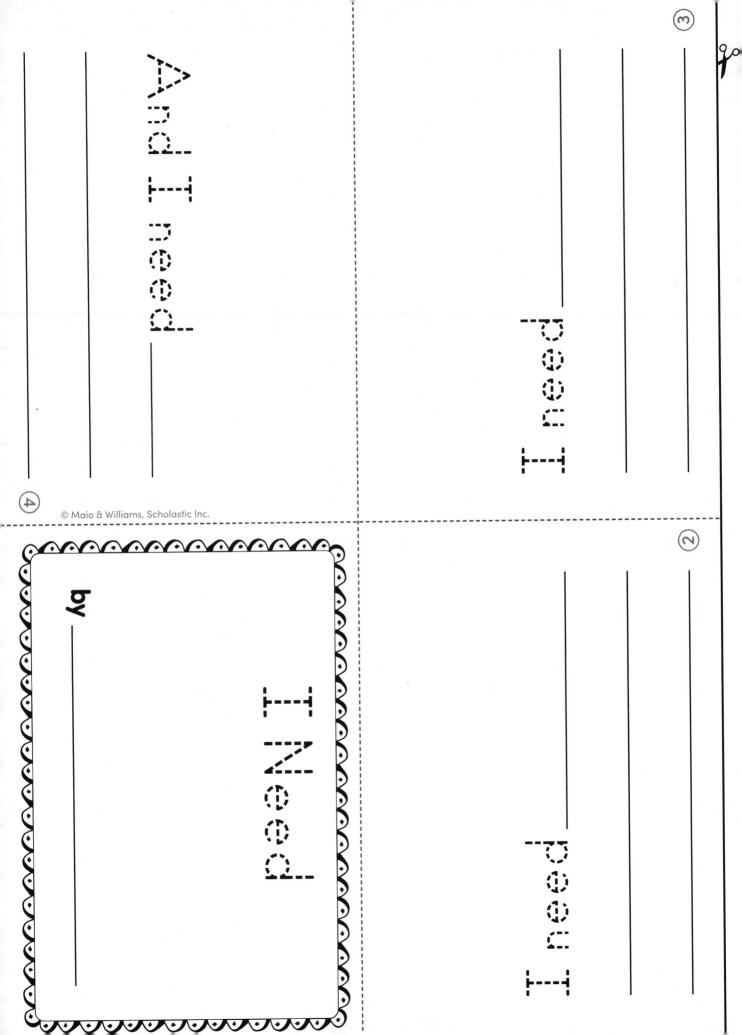

③

I need
_____

I need
_____

④

© Maio & Williams, Scholastic Inc.

And I need
_____

I Need

by _____

②

I need
_____

I need
_____

Who Lives In?

by ____

Who lives in ____

Who lives in ____

Who lives in ____

② ③ ④

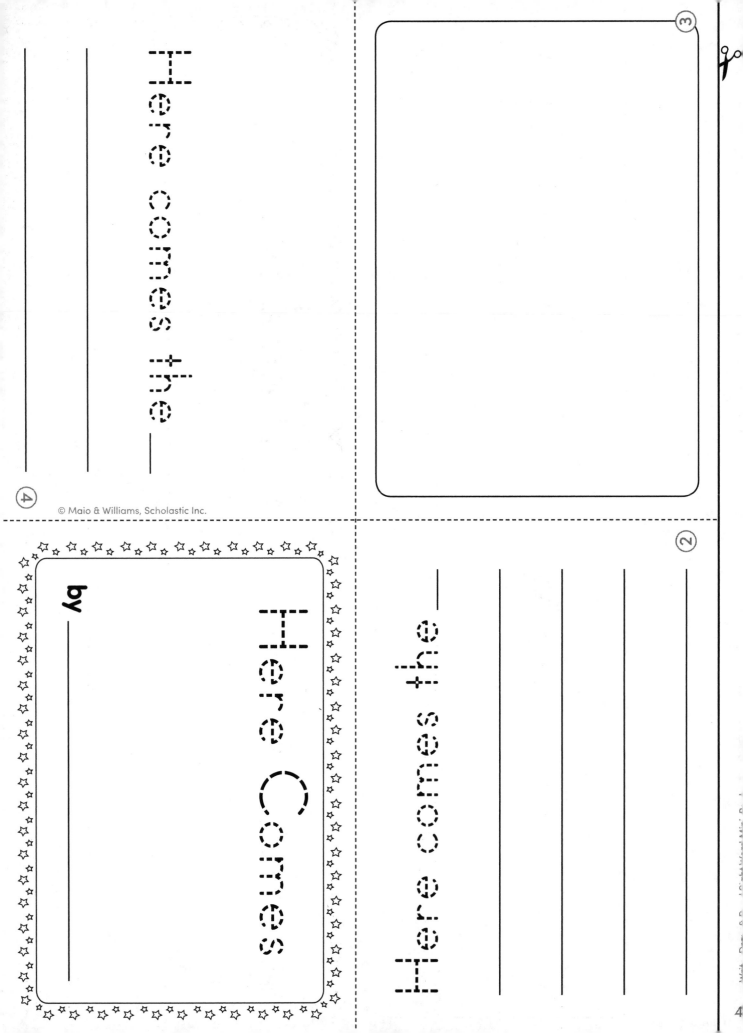

③

④

Here comes the ___

© Maio & Williams, Scholastic Inc.

②

Here comes the ___

Here Comes

by ___

Here comes the ___

48

Please _____

Help Me Find

by _____

Help me find _____

3

2

4

She Has Many

by ——

She has many ——

She has many ——

③

②

④

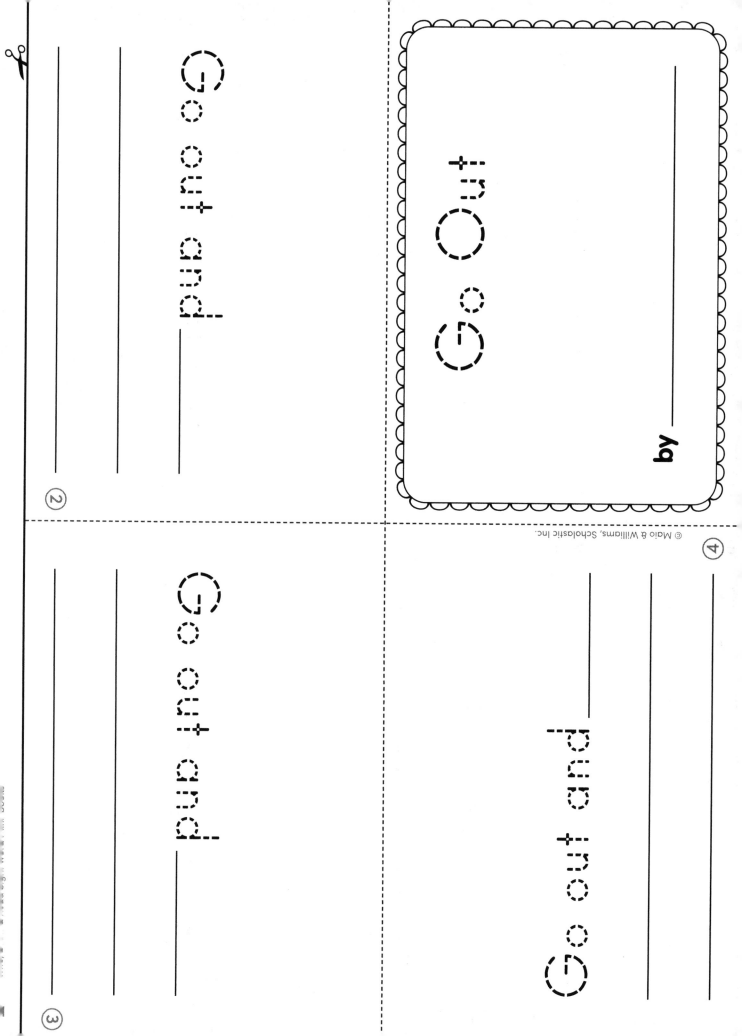

Go out and ___

②

Go out and ___

③

Go Out!

by ___

④

Go out and ___

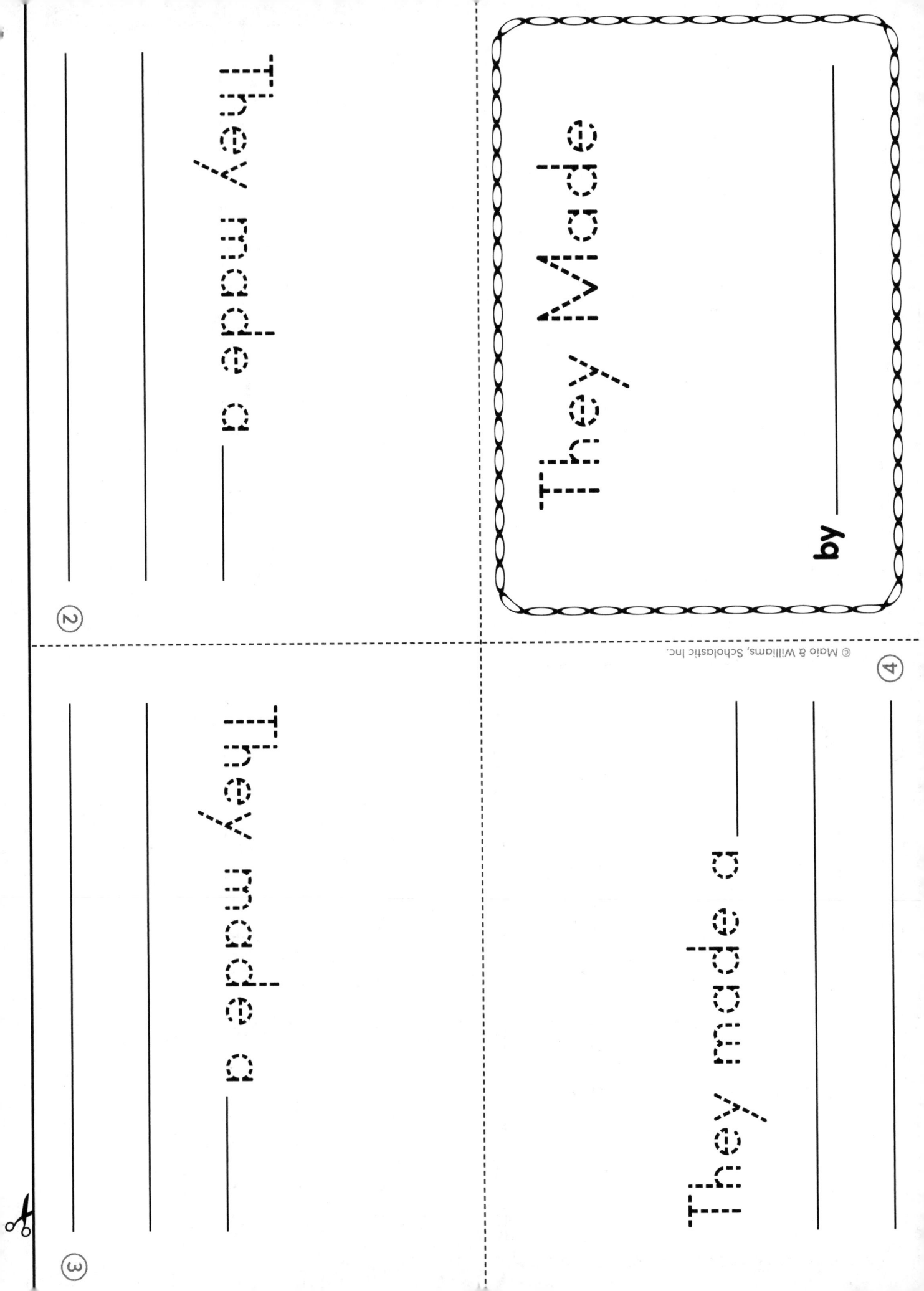

They Made

by ___

They made a ___

2

They made a ___

3

They made a ___

4

We could make _____

© Maio & Williams, Scholastic Inc.

④

③

We could make _____

②

We Could Make

by _____

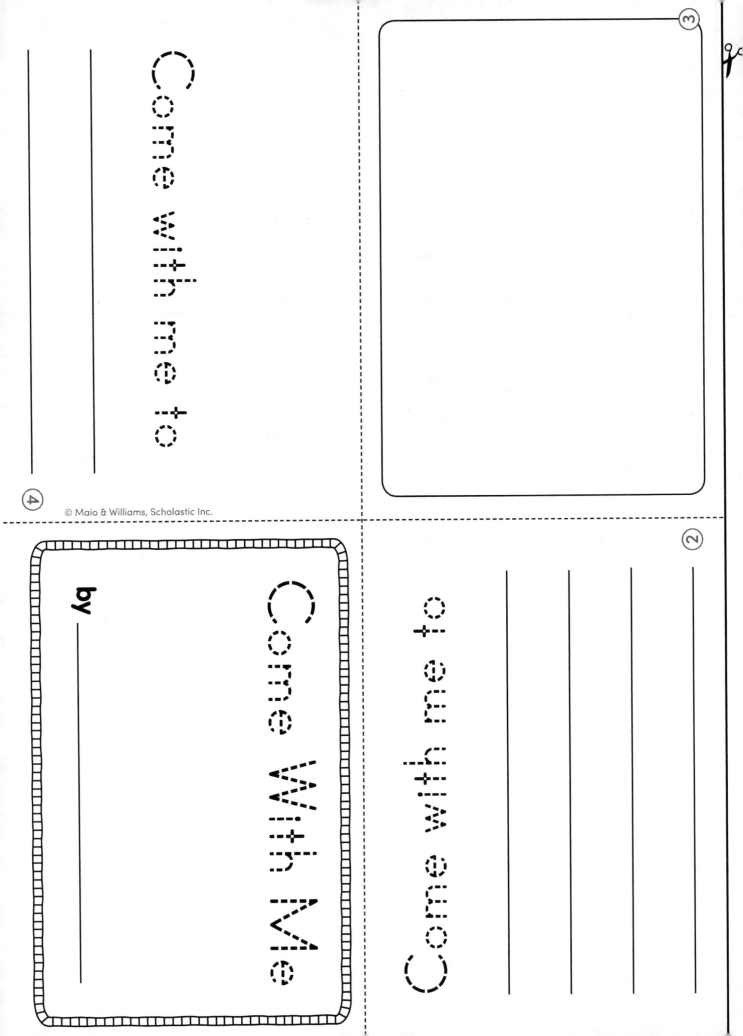

4

Come with me to

Come with me to

Come With Me

by

I Will Read

by _____

___ I will read to _____ ②

___ I will read to _____ ③

___ I will read to _____ ④

Would You Like? _____

by _____

Would you like _____

2

3

4

Would you like _____

Name: _____

SIGHT WORD PHRASES ASSESSMENT

Check the box if the child can read the sight word phrase.

- [ ] I can
- [ ] it is
- [ ] I am
- [ ] they are all
- [ ] I like
- [ ] are you
- [ ] I see the
- [ ] he can go
- [ ] come and get
- [ ] here is a
- [ ] do you like
- [ ] I will be
- [ ] it is in
- [ ] she was
- [ ] we have
- [ ] if you
- [ ] look at my

- [ ] they were
- [ ] this is his
- [ ] that is my
- [ ] where is the
- [ ] I saw her
- [ ] I will not
- [ ] they want
- [ ] these are for
- [ ] we ran from
- [ ] how do you
- [ ] one day I
- [ ] that was so
- [ ] we went into
- [ ] your mom said
- [ ] we can use
- [ ] when can we
- [ ] it is time

- [ ] some of us
- [ ] they had some
- [ ] he did not
- [ ] what is on
- [ ] there are two
- [ ] I need
- [ ] who lives in
- [ ] here comes the
- [ ] help me find
- [ ] she has many
- [ ] go out and
- [ ] they made a
- [ ] we could make
- [ ] come with me to
- [ ] I will read to
- [ ] would you like

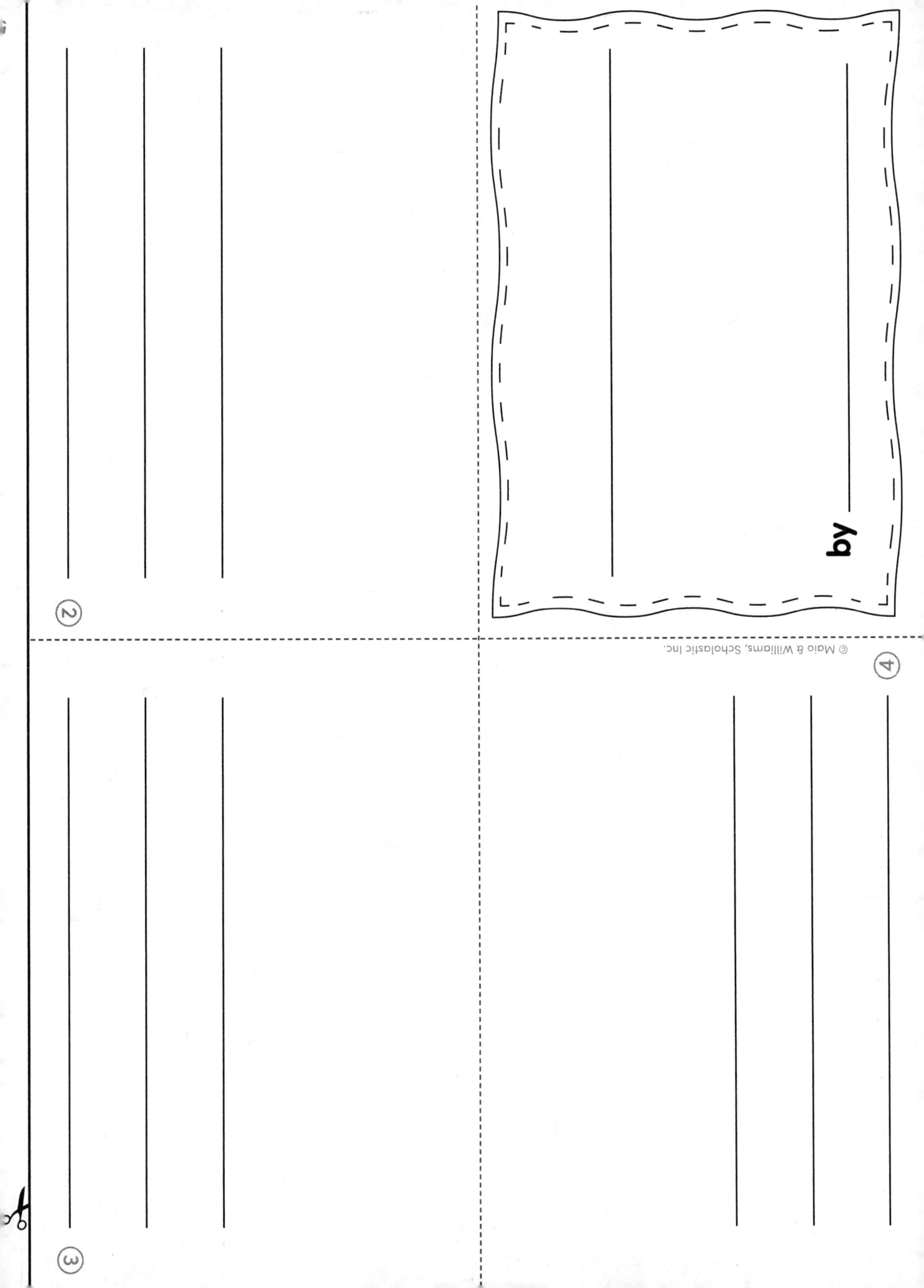

② ③ ④

by

by

_____

by

② ③ ④

④

by

②

②

③

④

by

④

②

by

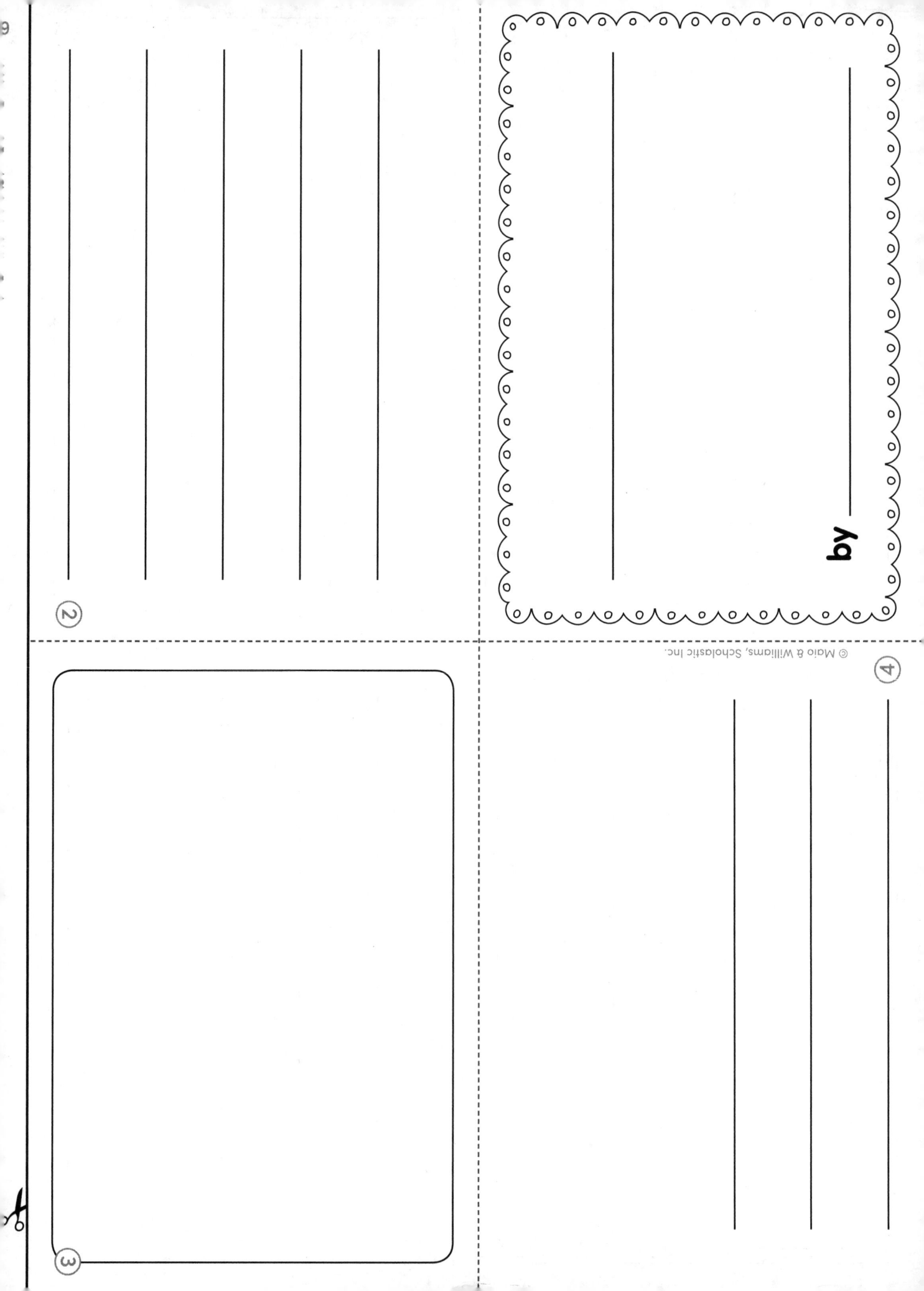

② ③ ④

by